MU
CHOCONUVO CREATIONS

Delicious and Easy Ways to Enjoy the Heart Healthy Benefits of ChocoNuvo

Muriel Angot
with Andrew Lessman

Recipes & Photography: Muriel Angot
Front Cover Photograph: Eric Cotsen
Back Cover Photograph: Eric Cotsen
Sous Chefs: Jesusita Montes & Miriam Araiza
Assistants: Kyle Klein & Newi Keser
Art Direction: Edward Moss

Published by the Andrew Lessman Foundation
430 Parkson Road, Henderson, NV 89011

Printed in the United States of America.

First Printing, April 2017

ISBN 978-0-9961765-1-4

Healthy recipes from our hearts to yours.

ABOUT THE AUTHOR

Muriel Angot was born and raised in the world's center of fine cuisine – Paris, France; however, would take Muriel a couple of decades to rediscover her Parisian culinary roots, since she initia followed in her parents' footsteps studying Fine Art at the Sorbonne University in Paris. After colleg Muriel's innate curiosity and desire to explore the world saw her leave France, spending time Australia, Fiji, New Zealand and South America, until she fell in love with the United States where s established a beauty and wellness business in Aspen, Colorado. It wasn't until Muriel chose to atte cooking school that her true passion captured her and since that time, has never let go.

Like many French families, all the members of Muriel's family take pride in their abilities in the kitche But, it was Muriel's paternal grandmother, Simone, who had the greatest influence, since she was the ch and owner of a restaurant in Picardie, France – a small city in the countryside just outside Paris. Some Muriel's fondest childhood memories are of helping her grandmother create all the classic French dish that were served at her restaurant. The special moments she shared with her grandmother in the cultura rich environment of an authentic French kitchen helped to shape the rest of Muriel's life.

When Muriel moved from Colorado to California, the move presented an opportunity for a career change and, with great trepidati she decided to take the plunge. Despite hearing how challenging it would be, Muriel followed her dream and attended Le Cord Bleu cooking school in Paris – the same school attended by Julia Child. Ultimately, she graduated #1 in her class and now conside herself blessed to combine her two greatest passions – cooking and wellness.

Muriel's five previous cookbooks have been dedicated to making healthy eating a delicious and enjoyable pursuit. She endeavors reinvent classic recipes while also reintroducing Americans to healthy ingredients that so many of us have never previously enjoy or simply have long ago forgotten. This, her most recent cookbook, provides simple suggestions on how to make the benefits the world's most heart healthy and delicious dark chocolate readily available to everyone.

Bon appétit!

merica, chocolate is typically consumed as milk chocolate and found in candy, fections, cakes and desserts. It is almost always mixed with a long list of ıer" ingredients, with the most common being: milk, cream, flour, eggs and, ve all, abundant amounts of sugar. Although chocolate has been treasured centuries, in recent years, it has earned the respect of the scientific and dical community for its extensive health benefits. These benefits originate ı the cocoa bean itself, which is why the healthiest way to consume chocolate s a dark chocolate, a high percentage extract of the cocoa bean. **ChocoNuvo** recisely that. It is only available as a rich, dark chocolate with your choice of 3 erent intensities: 66%, 74% and 91%. All three intensities possess high levels hocolate's protective compounds. In terms of our health, it is unfortunate that st Americans prefer creamy milk chocolate and avoid the perceived dryness l bitterness of dark chocolate.

wever, **ChocoNuvo** is different. Although it is a true dark chocolate, it possesses a unique, natural cholesterol-lowering redient that provides the same creamy texture of milk chocolate – even in our 91% extreme dark chocolate! We accomplish s without adding milk, flour or other ingredients. In fact, a 26-calorie square of our 91% **ChocoNuvo** contains less than f a gram of sugar (less than 1/8 of a teaspoon). Of course, **ChocoNuvo** is delicious on its own, but it is that same uniquely amy texture and lack of bitterness that makes it ideal for cooking. Please feel free to get creative with some of Muriel's ipes that use **ChocoNuvo** in any of your own favorite recipes. You will love it! And, best of all, **ChocoNuvo** turns every ipe into a delicious, but powerful, cholesterol-lowering treat.

...ew Muriel

TABLE OF CONTENTS

Nutrition Information			
Serving Size **½ Cup**		Servings **2**	
Calories	**98**	Potassium	**52 mg**
Calories from fat	**54**	Total Carbohydrates	**10 g**
Total Fat	**6 g**	Dietary Fiber	**3 g**
Cholesterol	**0 mg**	Sugars	**2 g**
Sodium	**84 mg**	Protein	**1 g**
Vitamin A	**11 %**	Vitamin B2	**19 %**
Vitamin C	**1 %**	Vitamin B6	**1 %**
Calcium	**26 %**	Vitamin B12	**65 %**
Iron	**6 %**	Phosphorus	**2 %**
Vitamin D	**7 %**	Magnesium	**4 %**
Vitamin E	**24 %**	Zinc	**14 %**
Vitamin K	**2 %**	Copper	**5 %**

Other Beneficial Nutrients (per serving)	
Choline	**2 mg**
Phytosterols	**1,300 mg**

Hot Cocoa Angelina Style

2 "Demi-Tasses" • Prep Time: 5 minutes • Cooking Time: 7 minutes • Easy

One of my favorite spots in Paris is a restaurant and patisserie called Angelina, renowned for it's "world famous" hot chocolate. My mom used to take me there when I was a child and it's still a very special place for us. It has now become one of Andrew's favorites, so I took on his challenge to recreate Angelina's famous hot cocoa. Use any milk you like –the secret is to thicken it with a little cornstarch. I love the healthy spices and there is NO ADDITIONAL SUGAR added!

- 1 cup unsweetened almond milk or skim milk
- 1 clove
- 2 cinnamon sticks
- 1 vanilla bean
- 4 pieces ChocoNuvo
- 1 tbsp. cornstarch + 1 tbsp. water
- 2 star anise (to decorate)

---

1. In a small saucepan over medium heat, combine the milk, clove, 1 cinnamon stick and vanilla bean. Reduce to low heat and gently simmer for about 5 minutes, but DO NOT BOIL!

2. In a small bowl, mix the cornstarch with the water. Add to the warm milk, and add the ChocoNuvo. Mix with a whisk for about 2 minutes. Almost bring to a boil. Turn down the heat and let everything simmer together for a minute.

3. Pour the hot cocoa into 2 "demi-tasses" (2 half cups). Decorate with the star anise, the other cinnamon stick and/or vanilla bean and serve with our Coconut Cream *(page 43)*, if you wish to be decadent.

HEALTHY "MENDIANTS"

About 20 Small Pieces • Prep Time: 5 minutes • Cooling Time: 15 minutes • Very Eas

This is a French classic. They're called "mendiants" (the French word for beggars) because the represent the 4 "mendicants" or Monastic orders. It's so simple and goes perfectly with a cu of tea or coffee, or as a small treat after a meal. They are also a great "dessert" to serve gues without all the calories and sugar of dessert. I like to use a variety of nuts, seeds, candied ging and orange slices, dried figs, cranberries and lemon rinds. Feel free to be creative!

---

10 pieces ChocoNuvo

¾ cup mixed nuts and dried fruits, thinly sliced

Parchment paper

---

1 In a small bowl, melt the ChocoNuvo in the microwave for 45 seconds. Stir with spatula and add 15 more seconds at a time, until the chocolate is melted, stirrir in between. I take my time so it doesn't burn the precious ChocoNuvo.

2 Using the back of a spoon, spread approximately ½ tsp. of melted ChocoNuvo 1 inch diameter circles on the parchment paper. Place the nuts, seeds, and slice dried fruits on top of each round.

3 Place in the freezer for 15 min or longer, until the Mendiants are hardened. Wh they are done, they will come off the parchment paper very easily. I keep them the freezer, in a sealed container. Enjoy!

Nutrition Information

Serving Size **1 Piece** Servings **20**

Calories	**37**	Potassium	**36 mg**
Calories from fat	**27**	Total Carbohydrates	**3 g**
Total Fat	**3 g**	Dietary Fiber	**1 g**
Cholesterol	**0 mg**	Sugars	**1 g**
Sodium	**12 mg**	Protein	**1 g**
Iron	**1 %**	Vitamin B6	**1 %**
Vitamin E	**3 %**	Phosphorus	**2 %**
Vitamin K	**1 %**	Magnesium	**3 %**
Vitamin B1	**1 %**	Zinc	**2 %**
Vitamin B2	**1 %**	Copper	**5 %**
Niacin	**1 %**		

OTHER BENEFICIAL NUTRIENTS (PER SERVING)

Choline	**20 mg**
Phytosterols	**325 mg**

"BBF" (Banana, Berry Fun)

1 BBF • Prep Time: 6 minutes • Very Easy

This works for me as a very healthy breakfast - appetizing, simple to create and extremely healthy! Your kids will love it too and they can even help you make it. The banana and berries are rich in protective nutrients and yogurt is an excellent source of protein. We tend to use fat-free yogurt, coconut yogurt or our Sweet Cashew Paste [page 42]. Andrew loves the mild flavor and creamy texture of sheep yogurt. Feel free to make this your own creation and you can even top with our Coconut Cream [page 43].

- 1 banana
- 1 tbsp. plain, nonfat yogurt
- ¼ cup fruits (I used blueberries and pomegranates)
- 2 pieces ChocoNuvo
- 5-6 mint leaves

---

1. Peel and cut the banana in half. Place on your plate.
2. Spread the yogurt evenly on top of each banana half.
3. Decorate with fruits.
4. In a small bowl, melt the ChocoNuvo for 1 minute in the microwave and stir with a spatula. Drizzle the melted ChocoNuvo on top of the fruits with a teaspoon. Decorate with mint leaves and serve immediately.

Nutrition Information

Serving Size **1 BBF** — Servings **1**

Calories	**187**	Potassium	**491 mg**
Calories from fat	**45**	Total Carbohydrates	**38 g**
Total Fat	**5 g**	Dietary Fiber	**6 g**
Cholesterol	**0 mg**	Sugars	**21 g**
Sodium	**13 mg**	Protein	**2 g**
Vitamin A	**1 %**	Vitamin B6	**35 %**
Vitamin C	**19 %**	Folic Acid	**7 %**
Calcium	**4 %**	Vitamin B12	**4 %**
Iron	**2 %**	Phosphorus	**8 %**
Vitamin E	**2 %**	Magnesium	**12 %**
Vitamin K	**10 %**	Zinc	**5 %**
Vitamin B1	**5 %**	Selenium	**3 %**
Vitamin B2	**13 %**	Copper	**13 %**
Niacin	**7 %**		

Other Beneficial Nutrients (per serving)

Choline	**16 mg**
Phytosterols	**1,300 mg**
ALA	**100 mg**

Frozen Hot Cocoa

2 Cups • Cooking and Cooling Time: 13 minutes • Easy

Frozen Hot Cocoa seems to be a new trend, so I created my own healthy version with ChocoNuv I make this with unsweetened almond milk or our Sweet Cashew Paste [page 42], but any mi of your choice works great. I only do a 1-cup serving because it is surprisingly rich! What a trea You can top it with Coconut Cream [page 43], and I like to add star anise or a cinnamon stic You can also top with a little extra shaved ChocoNuvo before serving.

---

1 cup unsweetened almond milk

3 pieces ChocoNuvo

1 tsp. vanilla extract

1 cup ice

1 pinch sea salt

1 cinnamon stick or star anise to decorate

Coconut Cream (optional)

---

1 In a small saucepan over medium heat, combine the milk, ChocoNuvo, vanil extract and stir with a whisk until all are melted together and the mixture is warr about 3 minutes. DO NOT BOIL. Place in the freezer for 10 minutes.

2 Mix in the blender with ice until smooth. Add the sea salt.

3 Serve with Coconut Cream and a star anise or cinnamon stick. I use a vegetab peeler to shave a few pieces of ChocoNuvo on top.

Nutrition Information

Serving Size **1 Cup** Servings **2**

Calories	**71**	Potassium	**34 mg**
Calories from fat	**45**	Total Carbohydrates	**5 g**
Total Fat	**5 g**	Dietary Fiber	**3 g**
Cholesterol	**0 mg**	Sugars	**2 g**
Sodium	**158 mg**	Protein	**1 g**
Vitamin A	**11 %**	Vitamin B2	**18 %**
Calcium	**24 %**	Vitamin B12	**65 %**
Iron	**4 %**	Phosphorus	**2 %**
Vitamin D	**7 %**	Magnesium	**3 %**
Vitamin E	**24 %**	Zinc	**13 %**
Vitamin K	**1 %**	Copper	**4 %**

Other Beneficial Nutrients (per serving)

Choline	**1 mg**
Phytosterols	**975 mg**

EGG WHITE CREPES WITH BANANA

6 Small Crepes • Prep Time: 10 minutes • Cooking Time: 5 minutes • Medium

Crepes are very thin pancakes. When we made crepes with my grandma in celebration of "La Chandeleure," we'd hold a gold coin in our left hand while we flipped our first crepe. If our crepe made it back in the pan perfectly, that meant we'd have money all year! We often made entire dinners serving only crepes: savory, with ham and cheese or mushroom; and dessert, with powdered sugar or melted chocolate and banana. Add a tbsp. of agave or maple syrup if you like them sweeter. Also, it is lovely to let a piece of ChocoNuvo melt inside your folded crepe and top with banana.

- 4 egg whites
- 3 tbsp. almond milk
- 1 tsp. vanilla extract
- 2 tbsp. garbanzo flour or flour of your choice
- ¼ tsp. baking powder
- A pinch of salt
- coconut oil spray
- 1 banana
- 4 pieces ChocoNuvo
- A few mint leaves and 6 raspberries to serve (optional)

---

1 In a medium bowl, whisk together the egg whites, milk, and vanilla. In a second bowl, sift and mix the flour with the baking powder then add to the egg white batter. Whisk well.

2 Spray a nonstick skillet with oil spray (repeat before each crepe), place over medium/high heat, and pour 3 tbsp of the crepe mixture in the pan. Reduce the heat to medium, cook for 2 minutes, flip and cook 2 more minutes. The crepes should look nice and golden.

3 Place on a serving plate. Fold it in fourths. Decorate with a sliced banana. Melt the 4 pieces of ChocoNuvo for 1 minute in the microwave. Mix with a spatula and drizzle the chocolate on the top of the crepe. You may also decorate with mint and raspberries, if you wish.

Nutrition Information

Serving Size **2 Crepes** Servings **3**

Calories	142	Potassium	246 mg
Calories from fat	45	Total Carbohydrates	19 g
Total Fat	5 g	Dietary Fiber	3 g
Cholesterol	0 mg	Sugars	8 g
Sodium	179 mg	Protein	6 g
Vitamin A	2 %	Niacin	5 %
Vitamin C	8 %	Vitamin B6	12 %
Calcium	7 %	Folic Acid	7 %
Iron	3 %	Vitamin B12	12 %
Vitamin D	1 %	Phosphorus	5 %
Vitamin E	5 %	Magnesium	7 %
Vitamin K	2 %	Zinc	4 %
Vitamin B1	6 %	Selenium	20 %
Vitamin B2	26 %	Copper	7 %

OTHER BENEFICIAL NUTRIENTS (PER SERVING)

Choline	6 mg
Phytosterols	867 mg

Nutrition Information

Serving Size **¾ Cup** Servings **4**

Calories	**256**	Potassium	**320 mg**
Calories from fat	**144**	Total Carbohydrates	**26 g**
Total Fat	**16 g**	Dietary Fiber	**4 g**
Cholesterol	**0 mg**	Sugars	**12 g**
Sodium	**16 mg**	Protein	**6 g**
Vitamin A	**2 %**	Vitamin B6	**19 %**
Vitamin C	**36 %**	Folic Acid	**20 %**
Calcium	**3 %**	Vitamin B12	**15 %**
Iron	**14 %**	Phosphorus	**23 %**
Vitamin E	**4 %**	Magnesium	**28 %**
Vitamin K	**17 %**	Zinc	**26 %**
Vitamin B1	**11 %**	Selenium	**8 %**
Vitamin B2	**13 %**	Copper	**83 %**
Niacin	**9 %**		

OTHER BENEFICIAL NUTRIENTS (PER SERVING)

Choline	**63 mg**
Phytosterols	**325 mg**
ALA	**100 mg**

CASHEW CREAM BERRY BLISS

4 Small Bowls • Prep Time: 5 minutes • Easy

This is a great way to make a delicious, healthy smoothie – perfect anytime. I used our Coco Cream [page 43] and topped it with pomegranate seeds, bee pollen (for extra nutrien flaxseeds, chia seeds, granola, shaved ChocoNuvo and hemp seeds. Be creative and use berries or fruits you have at home, frozen too!

---

1 cup Sweet Cashew Paste *[page 42]*

1 cup frozen berries of your choice

2 pieces ChocoNuvo

½ cup pomegranate seeds

2 tsp. bee pollen

2 tbsp. granola

1 piece ChocoNuvo (optional for garnish)

1 tsp. Coconut Cream on each (optional)

---

1. In a blender, mix the frozen berries and ChocoNuvo with Sweet Cashew Pas adding 1 tbsp. of water at a time until it reaches your desired consistency. D NOT add too much water at one time! Divide evenly into each bowl.

2. Decorate with pomegranate seeds, bee pollen, granola (or anything else y wish), and shave little pieces of ChocoNuvo with a vegetable peeler and place top. Serve and enjoy immediately. You can top it with a little Coconut Cream, but mindful of the calories.

ChocoNuvo Mug Cake

1 Cake • Prep Time: 4 minutes • Cooking Time: 2-4 minutes • Easy

The hardest part about making my ChocoNuvo mug cake is waiting until it cools off. It looks and smells so delicious; I just can't wait to enjoy it. You can use any flour and milk of your choice. You can also replace the oat bran with another flour. I sometimes use a mix of blueberries, strawberries, and tropical fruits. Simply use what you will enjoy.

---

2 egg whites (or 1 whole egg)

1 tbsp. gluten-free baking flour

1 tbsp. Ultimate Oat Bran

1 tbsp. flaxseeds

1 tsp. baking powder

1 tsp. agave syrup

1 tsp. vanilla extract

¼ cup unsweetened almond milk

3 pieces ChocoNuvo

8 fresh raspberries

---

1. In a small bowl, whisk together the egg whites, flour, oat bran, flaxseeds, baking powder, agave syrup and vanilla extract. Add the milk and whisk well.
2. Melt the ChocoNuvo for 45 seconds to 1 minute in the microwave and stir it in to the batter.
3. Place 5 raspberries in a microwaveable mug and pour the batter on top (you can also mix the raspberries into the batter, if you prefer). Microwave for 2 minutes. Depending on your microwave, you might have to add up to an additional 2 minutes. Let it rest for 10 minutes.
4. Decorate with the remaining 3 raspberries. Eat immediately. Breakfast of champions!

Nutrition Information

Serving Size **1 Cake** Servings **1**

Calories	**298**	Potassium	**373 mg**
Calories from fat	**99**	Total Carbohydrates	**37 g**
Total Fat	**11 g**	Dietary Fiber	**9 g**
Cholesterol	**1 mg**	Sugars	**16 g**
Sodium	**627 mg**	Protein	**13 g**
Vitamin A	**6 %**	Niacin	**8 %**
Vitamin C	**13 %**	Vitamin B6	**9 %**
Calcium	**39 %**	Folic Acid	**11 %**
Iron	**9 %**	Vitamin B12	**15 %**
Vitamin D	**5 %**	Phosphorus	**36 %**
Vitamin E	**3 %**	Magnesium	**19 %**
Vitamin K	**6 %**	Zinc	**11 %**
Vitamin B1	**24 %**	Selenium	**37 %**
Vitamin B2	**44 %**	Copper	**20 %**

Other Beneficial Nutrients (per serving)

Choline	**23 mg**
Phytosterols	**1,950 mg**
ALA	**2,100 mg**

GAIL'S VERY CHOCONUVO BANANA BREA

15 Thin Slices • Prep Time: 20 minutes • Cooking Time: 50 minutes • Medium

Andrew's sister, Gail, gave me this wonderful recipe and I decided to adapt it with ChocoNu Use ripe bananas as they are the sweetest. This is great as a breakfast bread with almond but and jam. You can crush the ChocoNuvo in a mortar or process in a Cuisinart. Frozen ChocoNu works best, since it will grind into chips instead of melting. I serve it with fresh, beautiful cut fru

---

- Cooking oil spray
- 1 banana to decorate
- ½ cup Earth Balance Butter (softened)
- ½ cup light brown sugar (or coconut sugar)
- 1 tsp. vanilla extract
- 1 cup mashed banana (2 to 3 ripe bananas)
- 2 eggs (or 4 egg whites)
- 1½ cups gluten-free baking flour
- 1 tsp. baking soda
- 1 tsp. baking powder
- ½ tsp. salt
- ½ cup fat free sour cream
- 12 pieces ChocoNuvo (crushed)

---

1. Preheat the oven to 350° and spray a loaf pan with cooking oil. Slice a banana half lengthwise and arrange it across the bottom in a design of your choice.

2. In a medium to large bowl, use a spatula to cream the butter and sugar until forms a smooth paste. Add the vanilla, mashed bananas and eggs. Mix well!

3. In a smaller bowl, sift together the flour, baking powder, baking soda and sal Combine the wet and dry ingredients, blend in the sour cream, and fold in th crushed ChocoNuvo. Pour the batter evenly in the loaf pan.

4. Bake for 45 to 50 minutes, until a toothpick inserted in the bread comes out clear Remove from the oven and let it cool for 15 minutes or more. Serve with cut fruit and nut butter!

Nutrition Information

Serving Size **1 Slice** — Servings **15**

Calories	171	Potassium	130 mg
Calories from fat	72	Total Carbohydrates	23 g
Total Fat	8 g	Dietary Fiber	2 g
Cholesterol	1 mg	Sugars	9 g
Sodium	278 mg	Protein	3 g
Vitamin A	1 %	Vitamin B6	7 %
Vitamin C	3 %	Folic Acid	11 %
Calcium	4 %	Vitamin B12	1 %
Iron	4 %	Phosphorus	5 %
Vitamin E	7 %	Magnesium	4 %
Vitamin B1	10 %	Zinc	2 %
Vitamin B2	12 %	Selenium	12 %
Niacin	7 %	Copper	5 %

OTHER BENEFICIAL NUTRIENTS (PER SERVING)

Choline	5 mg
Phytosterols	520 mg
ALA	400 mg

GLUTEN-FREE PANCAKES

6 Small Pancakes • Prep Time: 5 minutes • Cooking Time: 7 minutes • Easy

I have made these healthy pancakes for 12 years and still love them. The crushed ChocoNuvo makes them even tastier. I sometimes use cottage cheese instead of applesauce and add a tbsp. of agave or maple syrup if the pancakes are not sweet enough. I mix the batter in a blender for a smoother consistency. I used pomegranate seeds here but use any fruits or toppings you have at home!

½ cup gluten-free flour

½ cup Ultimate Oat Bran

½ cup unsweetened applesauce

4 egg whites (or 2 eggs)

½ tsp. baking soda

½ tsp. baking powder

1 tbsp. flaxseed

2 tbsp. milk (of your choice)

1 tsp. vanilla extract

1 tsp. cinnamon

4 pieces ChocoNuvo (Crushed into chips)

Cooking oil spray

---

1 Whisk together the flour, oat bran, applesauce, eggs, baking soda, baking powder, flaxseed, milk, vanilla extract and cinnamon in a bowl, or in a blender for a smoother batter. Mix in the crushed ChocoNuvo chips.

2 Lightly spray a skillet with cooking oil (sometimes I use coconut oil) and place over medium to high heat. Pour ¼ cup of batter in the pan and turn the heat down to medium. Cook for about 3 minutes. Flip to the other side and cook for another 3 minutes, or until the pancakes are golden brown. This should make about 6 small pancakes.

3 Serve with your choice of fruits and maple syrup.

Nutrition Information

Serving Size **1 Pancake** Servings **6**

Calories	122	Potassium	130 mg
Calories from fat	27	Total Carbohydrates	19 g
Total Fat	3 g	Dietary Fiber	3 g
Cholesterol	0 mg	Sugars	3 g
Sodium	185 mg	Protein	5 g
Calcium	5 %	Vitamin B12	2 %
Iron	4 %	Phosphorus	6 %
Vitamin B1	10 %	Magnesium	4 %
Vitamin B2	15 %	Zinc	2 %
Niacin	5 %	Selenium	16 %
Vitamin B6	2 %	Copper	5 %
Folic Acid	8 %		

OTHER BENEFICIAL NUTRIENTS (PER SERVING)

Choline	4 mg
Phytosterols	433 mg
ALA	400 mg

Grilled Mango with ChocoNuvo and Cookie

4 Servings • Prep Time: 10 minutes • Grilling Time: 7 minutes • Easy

I love to create recipes with the most nutrient-rich foods. This lovely dessert is as beautiful a it is healthy! Replace the mango with any fruit of your choice. In France, we use orange liqueu but a reduced calorie orange juice or fresh fruit puree is a healthier version. I like to top it wit crumbles of my "Chouette Oatmeal Cookies" [page 25] but a Biscotti works well too.

- 2 ripe mangos cut in half, pit removed
- 1 tbsp. honey
- 2 tbsp. orange liqueur or orange juice (optional)
- 4 pieces ChocoNuvo
- 1 "Chouette Oatmeal Cookie" or biscotti, crushec
- 1 lime, cut in 8 pieces

---

1 Preheat the broiler. Score the mango halves with 2 or 3 shallow crosshatched line and arrange on a baking sheet. Drizzle a little honey and liqueur on the mang pieces and broil for approximately 6 to 7 minutes, until nicely browned. This may tak less time, depending on your broiler.

2 Place the grilled mango on your serving plate.

3 Melt the ChocoNuvo for 1 minute maximum in the microwave. Use a spatula t mix well. Drizzle on top of the mango to decorate. Sprinkle a little of the crushe cookie on each mango half. Garnish with lime and zest, and serve immediately.

Nutrition Information

Serving Size **½ Mango** — Servings **4**

Calories	**140**	Potassium	**214 mg**
Calories from fat	**27**	Total Carbohydrates	**29 g**
Total Fat	**3 g**	Dietary Fiber	**3 g**
Cholesterol	**3 mg**	Sugars	**22 g**
Sodium	**23 mg**	Protein	**2 g**
Vitamin A	**8 %**	Niacin	**7 %**
Vitamin C	**60 %**	Vitamin B6	**11 %**
Calcium	**3 %**	Folic Acid	**14 %**
Iron	**3 %**	Phosphorus	**5 %**
Vitamin E	**8 %**	Magnesium	**4 %**
Vitamin K	**6 %**	Zinc	**2 %**
Vitamin B1	**6 %**	Selenium	**5 %**
Vitamin B2	**6 %**	Copper	**15 %**

Other Beneficial Nutrients (per serving)

Choline	**11 mg**
Phytosterols	**650 mg**

Nutrition Information

Serving Size **1 Piece** | Servings **14**

Calories	**27**	Potassium	**3 mg**
Calories from fat	**9**	Total Carbohydrates	**3 g**
Total Fat	**1 g**	Dietary Fiber	**1 g**
Cholesterol	**0 mg**	Sugars	**1 g**
Sodium	**17 mg**	Protein	**0 g**
Vitamin A	**2 %**	Niacin	**5 %**
Vitamin C	**2 %**	Vitamin B6	**3 %**
Iron	**4 %**	Folic Acid	**6 %**
Vitamin B1	**4 %**	Vitamin B12	**5 %**
Vitamin B2	**6 %**	Selenium	**1 %**

OTHER BENEFICIAL NUTRIENTS (PER SERVING)

Phytosterols . . . . **464 mg**

MINI RICE CRISPY TREATS

About 14 Mini Treats • Prep Time: 10 minutes • Cooling Time: 1 hour • Very Easy

These are fun and easy to make, and they can be served with coffee or tea or after any meal as a healthy and low-calorie dessert. I was able to find organic, gluten-free rice crispy cereal without added sugar, but you can use whatever is available.

- 10 pieces ChocoNuvo
- 1 cup rice crispy cereal
- 14 small muffin liners
- 14 toothpicks (optional)

1 Melt the ChocoNuvo in a small to medium bowl for 1 minute in the microwave. Mix with a spatula. You might want to heat for 15 more seconds if needed. Don't overdo it as it will burn the ChocoNuvo!

2 Add the rice crispy cereal and mix well, until all the rice is coated. Put 1 tsp. in each muffin liner. I add a little toothpick so it's easier to eat. Freeze for at least 1 hour.

TARTELETTES WITH SWEET CASHEW CREAM

24 Mini Tartelettes • Prep Time: 30 minutes • Cooling Time: 1 hour • Difficult

This recipe is a little time consuming but worth every minute. You can use pecans or walnu I use our Sweet Cashew Paste [page 42] for an all-vegan recipe.

Crust:

¾ cup pecans (or walnuts)

¾ cup dates

1 tsp. coconut oil

½ cup Ultimate Oatmeal

1 tbsp. agave

6 pieces ChocoNuvo

A pinch of salt

Filling:

½ cup of Sweet Cashew Paste *(page 42)*

¾ cup berries (I use frozen raspberries)

24 mini muffin liners

1 In a high-quality food processor, mix the pecans, dates (pits removed), coconu oil, agave, salt, oatmeal and the 6 pieces of ChocoNuvo. Process until it forms dough. If needed, you can add a tbsp. of water.

2 Line the muffin tins and press 1 tsp. of dough at the bottom so it forms a crust. make a thumb print at the bottom to place the filling. Place in the freezer for abou 30 minutes, and during this time make the cashew paste.

3 Mix the Sweet Cashew Paste and the frozen berries in a blender until nice and smooth.

4 Remove the dough from the freezer and place ½ tbsp. of the filling on each sma crust. You can use a pastry tube and a bag, but a spoon works just fine. Place i the freezer for a minimum of 30 minutes.

5 Decorate with blueberries, raspberries, pomegranate seeds, strawberries c other garnish of your choice. You can also melt 2 or 3 pieces of ChocoNuvo in th microwave and drizzle some on top.

Nutrition Information

Serving Size **1 Tartelette** Servings **24**

Calories	73	Potassium	76 mg
Calories from fat	36	Total Carbohydrates	8 g
Total Fat	4 g	Dietary Fiber	2 g
Cholesterol	0 mg	Sugars	5 g
Sodium	7 mg	Protein	1 g
Vitamin C	2 %	Vitamin B6	2 %
Calcium	1 %	Folic Acid	1 %
Iron	2 %	Phosphorus	4 %
Vitamin E	1 %	Magnesium	4 %
Vitamin K	2 %	Zinc	4 %
Vitamin B1	3 %	Selenium	1 %
Vitamin B2	2 %	Copper	12 %
Niacin	1 %		

OTHER BENEFICIAL NUTRIENTS (PER SERVING)

Choline	8 mg
Phytosterols	163 mg

"IT'S PEACHEEE!"

4 Plates • Prep Time: 12 minutes • Cooking Time: 6 minutes • Easy

We received some lovely peaches from Andrew's mom, so I felt compelled to create a recipe that used them. Roasted pineapple can also work well. I added extra ChocoNuvo to the granola so it would melt on the grilled peaches. As an option, shredded coconut can also work well.

---

4 peaches

1 tsp. oil spray or coconut oil

½ cup granola

4 pieces ChocoNuvo (crushed)

2 tbsp. sliced almonds

1 tsp. agave nectar or honey

6 oz. plain, nonfat yogurt or Coconut Cream *(page 43)*

Edible flowers and/or mint leaves (optional)

---

1 Peel the peaches and cut them into slices. In a non-stick pan over high heat, melt the coconut oil and place the peaches in the pan. Drizzle with agave or honey and let it cook for 3 minutes. Flip the peaches and cook for another 3 minutes.

2 Mix the granola with the crushed pieces of ChocoNuvo.

3 Roast the sliced almonds for a couple of minutes in a skillet.

4 Plate the peaches and sprinkle the granola/ChocoNuvo mix over them Add a small amount of yogurt or Coconut Cream for a fancier dessert. Sprinkle the toasted almonds on top. Add the mint leaves and the edible flowers if you wish.

Nutrition Information

Serving Size **1 Plate** Servings **4**

Calories	**216**	Potassium	**474 mg**
Calories from fat	**81**	Total Carbohydrates	**29 g**
Total Fat	**9 g**	Dietary Fiber	**5 g**
Cholesterol	**1 mg**	Sugars	**20 g**
Sodium	**26 mg**	Protein	**6 g**
Vitamin A	**4 %**	Vitamin B6	**8 %**
Vitamin C	**14 %**	Folic Acid	**6 %**
Calcium	**9 %**	Vitamin B12	**7 %**
Iron	**7 %**	Phosphorus	**24 %**
Vitamin E	**26 %**	Magnesium	**19 %**
Vitamin K	**6 %**	Zinc	**16 %**
Vitamin B1	**16 %**	Selenium	**10 %**
Vitamin B2	**19 %**	Copper	**28 %**
Niacin	**12 %**		

OTHER BENEFICIAL NUTRIENTS (PER SERVING)

Choline	**23 mg**
Phytosterols	**650 mg**
ALA	**100 mg**

CHIA PUDDING WITH CLEMENTINES

2 Jars • Prep Time: 10 minutes • Resting Time: Overnight • Easy

I enjoy cooking with chia seeds because they are easy to work with and rich in vegetable-bas Omega 3s, protein, fiber and protective compounds. I use mason jars, but a small bowl or c can also do the trick. I often use coconut yogurt, colorful fruits, and sliced almonds to decora

---

- 1 cup unsweetened almond milk (or milk of your choice)
- ¼ cup whole chia seeds
- 1 tsp. maple syrup
- 1 tsp. vanilla extract
- ½ cup plain, nonfat yogurt (or coconut yogurt)
- 2 clementines
- 4 pieces ChocoNuvo

---

1 In a medium bowl, combine the milk, chia seeds, maple syrup and vanilla extrac and mix with a spoon until gently blended. Let it rest. I usually mix it again afte a half hour and then let it rest overnight in the fridge. It will then have the "puddin effect"! You can also mix half yogurt and half milk if you like it thicker and creamier. am watching my calories, so I only use milk.

2 The next day: Crush 2 pieces of ChocoNuvo and mix it with the pudding.

3 In the mason jar: peel your 2 clementines and place a few pieces at the bottom Add a little of the pudding, a little yogurt and a few more clementines until yo get the "layer effect".

4 Decorate with a couple more clementine pieces, add some yogurt on the to and shave the 2 other pieces of ChocoNuvo with a vegetable peeler, and add o top. Voila!

Nutrition Information

Serving Size **1 Jar** — Servings **2**

Calories	**303**	Potassium	**442 mg**
Calories from fat	**135**	Total Carbohydrates	**36 g**
Total Fat	**15 g**	Dietary Fiber	**14 g**
Cholesterol	**1 mg**	Sugars	**19 g**
Sodium	**134 mg**	Protein	**9 g**
Vitamin A	**16 %**	Vitamin B6	**8 %**
Vitamin C	**31 %**	Folic Acid	**9 %**
Calcium	**57 %**	Vitamin B12	**80 %**
Iron	**16 %**	Phosphorus	**52 %**
Vitamin D	**7 %**	Magnesium	**41 %**
Vitamin E	**25 %**	Zinc	**38 %**
Vitamin B1	**23 %**	Selenium	**33 %**
Vitamin B2	**44 %**	Copper	**37 %**
Niacin	**21 %**		

OTHER BENEFICIAL NUTRIENTS (PER SERVING)

Choline	**19 mg**
Phytosterols	**1,300 mg**
ALA	**5,100 mg**

ZUCCHINI MINI MUFFINS

About 24 Mini Muffins • Prep Time: 20 minutes • Cooking Time: 20 minutes • Medium

Who knew zucchini and chocolate could make for a perfect marriage?! Zucchini is low in calories and makes these muffins healthy and moist. You do not notice the taste of the zucchini, and its texture blends perfectly with the richness of ChocoNuvo.

Oil spray
¾ cup gluten-free baking flour
¾ cup Ultimate Oatmeal
½ cup almond flour
1 tsp. baking powder
1 tsp. baking soda
A pinch of salt
½ cup brown sugar
1 tsp. cinnamon
2 eggs
¾ cup nonfat milk (or milk of your choice)
¾ cup grated zucchini (about 1 small zucchini)
8 pieces ChocoNuvo, crushed

---

1 Preheat the oven to 350°. Place paper liners in a muffin tin and lightly spray with oil.

2 In a large bowl, mix the flour, oatmeal, almond flour, baking powder, baking soda, sugar, cinnamon and a pinch of salt. In a separate smaller bowl, combine the eggs and milk.

3 Fold the wet ingredients into the dry ingredients, being careful not to over mix. Grate the zucchini, squeeze it in a paper towel to remove excess water, and add it to the batter. You can save a little of the zucchini to decorate the top of the muffins, if you wish. Add in the crushed ChocoNuvo as well.

4 Divide the batter evenly among the muffin cups. Garnish with a tiny piece of zucchini. Bake for approximately 20 minutes, until the muffins are puffy and golden, and an inserted toothpick comes out clean.

Nutrition Information

Serving Size **1 Muffin** Servings **24**

Calories	**68**	Potassium	**51 mg**
Calories from fat	**27**	Total Carbohydrates	**10 g**
Total Fat	**3 g**	Dietary Fiber	**1 g**
Cholesterol	**14 mg**	Sugars	**4 g**
Sodium	**91 mg**	Protein	**2 g**
Vitamin A	**2 %**	Vitamin B6	**1 %**
Vitamin C	**1 %**	Folic Acid	**4 %**
Calcium	**4 %**	Vitamin B12	**3 %**
Iron	**2 %**	Phosphorus	**4 %**
Vitamin D	**1 %**	Magnesium	**1 %**
Vitamin B1	**3 %**	Zinc	**2 %**
Vitamin B2	**5 %**	Selenium	**5 %**
Niacin	**2 %**	Copper	**1 %**

OTHER BENEFICIAL NUTRIENTS (PER SERVING)

Choline	**13 mg**
Phytosterols	**217 mg**

Dipped Strawberries with Crushed Pistachios

10 Strawberries • Prep Time: 8 minutes • Cooling Time: 30 minutes • Very Easy

This is our version of chocolate fondue and one of the simplest recipes in this cookbo I sometimes dip our Chouette Oatmeal Cookies [page 25] and serve them with the fruits. It's n with coffee or tea or as a healthy dessert. Of course, it is low in calories and sugar.

---

10 whole strawberries	¼ cup crushed pistachios	10 toothpicks (optional)
5 pieces ChocoNuvo	Parchment paper	

---

1 Wash the strawberries and dry well. Cut the ends. Place each strawberry or toothpick.

2 Melt the ChocoNuvo for 1 minute in the microwave. Mix well with a small spatul Dip half of each berry first in the melted ChocoNuvo, and then in the pistachic (or you can sprinkle them on top).

3 Place each strawberry on the parchment paper and refrigerate for a minimum 30 minutes.

Nutrition Information

Serving Size **1 Strawberry** Servings **10**

Calories	**34**	Potassium	**49 mg**
Calories from fat	**18**	Total Carbohydrates	**3 g**
Total Fat	**2 g**	Dietary Fiber	**1 g**
Cholesterol	**0 mg**	Sugars	**1 g**
Sodium	**0 mg**	Protein	**1 g**
Vitamin C	**10 %**	Vitamin B6	**3 %**
Calcium	**1 %**	Folic Acid	**1 %**
Iron	**1 %**	Phosphorus	**2 %**
Vitamin E	**1 %**	Magnesium	**2 %**
Vitamin K	**1 %**	Zinc	**1 %**
Vitamin B1	**2 %**	Selenium	**1 %**
Vitamin B2	**1 %**	Copper	**5 %**
Niacin	**1 %**		

Other Beneficial Nutrients (per serving)

Choline	**3 mg**
Phytosterols	**325 mg**

"Chouette Oatmeal Cookies"

24 Cookies • Prep Time: 20 minutes • Cooking Time: 15 minutes • Medium

Since I started exploring cookies with our **"Oat"standing Recipes** *booklet, I have discovered all kinds of fun, healthy cookie recipes. I love to drizzle ChocoNuvo on top of these cookies for even richer flavor, as well as cholesterol-lowering power. In French, Chouette means AWESOME!*

- Coconut baking spray
- 1 cup Ultimate Oatmeal
- ¾ cup unsweetened almond milk
- 1 tsp. cinnamon
- 2 tbsp. flaxseeds
- 1 tsp. vanilla extract
- 1½ cups gluten-free baking flour
- 1 tsp. baking powder
- 1 tsp. baking soda
- ½ tsp. salt
- ⅓ cup oil (I use coconut oil)
- ⅓ cup brown sugar
- ¼ cup agave syrup
- 10 pieces ChocoNuvo (crushed)
- 2 pieces ChocoNuvo (melted)

---

1. Preheat the oven to 350°. Line a baking sheet with parchment paper or aluminum foil and coat lightly with coconut baking spray.

2. In a medium bowl, combine the oatmeal, milk, cinnamon, flaxseeds and vanilla extract. Let it rest. In a small bowl, mix the flour, baking powder, baking soda and salt. In a large bowl, mix the coconut oil, brown sugar and agave with an electric mixer.

3. Using a spatula, quickly fold a little of the flour mixture into the wet ingredients, then add a little of the oatmeal mixture, alternating until you incorporate all the ingredients. Do not overmix. The mixture should be quite thick. Fold the crushed ChocoNuvo into the mixture.

4. Form into 24 small balls (about 1 tbsp. each) and place on a lined baking sheet approximately 1½ inches apart. Bake for 13 to 15 minutes, until golden. After the cookies have cooled off, drizzle the additional melt ChocoNuvo on top.

Nutrition Information

Serving Size **1 Cookie** — Servings **24**

Calories	106	Potassium	34 mg
Calories from fat	45	Total Carbohydrates	15 g
Total Fat	5 g	Dietary Fiber	1 g
Cholesterol	0 mg	Sugars	5 g
Sodium	127 mg	Protein	1 g
Vitamin A	1 %	Niacin	4 %
Vitamin C	1 %	Vitamin B6	1 %
Calcium	3 %	Folic Acid	6 %
Iron	3 %	Vitamin B12	4 %
Vitamin D	1 %	Phosphorus	3 %
Vitamin E	2 %	Magnesium	2 %
Vitamin K	1 %	Zinc	2 %
Vitamin B1	7 %	Selenium	5 %
Vitamin B2	5 %	Copper	3 %

Other Beneficial Nutrients (per serving)

Choline	2 mg
Phytosterols	271 mg
ALA	200 mg

MINI PECAN BROWNIES

24 Mini Brownies • Prep Time: 20 minutes • Cooking Time: 18 minutes • Medium

This is a versatile recipe, as you can decorate it any way you like, with a little extra melt ChocoNuvo, fruits and/or nuts. Any flour works (I don't use coconut flour though), and any or even butter can replace the coconut oil.

Mini silicon baking mold

Coconut oil spray

⅔ cup coconut sugar (or brown sugar)

2 eggs

1 tsp. vanilla extract

15 pieces ChocoNuvo

½ cup coconut oil

½ cup+2 tbsp. flour, siftec (I used quinoa flour)

¼ cup pecans, crushed (plus a few whole pecans to decorate)

---

1 Preheat the oven to 350°. Spray the silicon baking mold very lighty (unless you u: the mini muffin tins with muffin liners).

2 In a medium bowl, beat the eggs with the sugar and vanilla until fluffy.

3 Melt the ChocoNuvo and the coconut oil together in the microwave for about minute. If you need to melt it for a little longer, only add 15 seconds at a time ar mix with a spatula. DO NOT burn the ChocoNuvo. Add the flour and pecans, and m well, but DO NOT over mix.

4 Place 1 tbsp. of mixture in each mold, and bake for 18 minutes or until an inserte toothpick comes out clean. Cool and decorate any way you wish.

Nutrition Information

Serving Size **1 Brownie** Servings **24**

Calories	**96**	Potassium	**19 mg**
Calories from fat	**63**	Total Carbohydrates	**8 g**
Total Fat	**7 g**	Dietary Fiber	**1 g**
Cholesterol	**14 mg**	Sugars	**5 g**
Sodium	**6 mg**	Protein	**1 g**
Vitamin A	**1 %**	Folic Acid	**3 %**
Calcium	**1 %**	Vitamin B12	**1 %**
Iron	**2 %**	Phosphorus	**2 %**
Vitamin B1	**3 %**	Magnesium	**1 %**
Vitamin B2	**3 %**	Zinc	**2 %**
Niacin	**2 %**	Selenium	**4 %**
Vitamin B6	**1 %**	Copper	**3 %**

OTHER BENEFICIAL NUTRIENTS (PER SERVING)

Choline	**12 mg**
Phytosterols	**406 mg**

BERRY BREAKFAST POPSICLES WITH GRANOLA

6 Popsicles • Prep Time: 15 minutes • Freezing Time: 12 hours • Easy

It adds calories, but you can also make a version of this using my Sweet Cashew Paste [page 42] and mix it with melted ChocoNuvo (for a marble effect). Berries are always very healthy and you can use your choice of yogurt. I used raspberries, blueberries and a kiwi. Anything you have can work!

---

6 oz. plain, nonfat yogurt (I used sheep yogurt)

1 cup berries (I used frozen)

1 kiwi

6 popsicle molds (⅓ cup each serving)

6 pieces ChocoNuvo

⅓ to ½ cup granola

---

1 Peel and cut the kiwi (I cut the slices in half).

2 In a medium bowl, combine the yogurt and berries, mashing the berries to add color. Do not over-mash!

3 Add the sliced kiwi at the bottom of a popsicle mold. Add the yogurt and berry mixture (about ⅓ cup per mold). Freeze overnight.

4 Melt the pieces of ChocoNuvo in the microwave for 1 minute. Mix with a spatula. Place the granola on a plate.

5 To remove each popsicle from the mold, simply run it under warm water for a second. Don't be impatient! Dip one side or the end of the popsicle in the ChocoNuvo and then dip right away in the granola. Eat immediately.

Nutrition Information

Serving Size **1 Popsicle** Servings **6**

Calories	112	Potassium	221 mg
Calories from fat	45	Total Carbohydrates	15 g
Total Fat	5 g	Dietary Fiber	3 g
Cholesterol	1 mg	Sugars	8 g
Sodium	26 mg	Protein	3 g
Vitamin C	36 %	Vitamin B6	5 %
Calcium	7 %	Folic Acid	5 %
Iron	4 %	Vitamin B12	7 %
Vitamin E	9 %	Phosphorus	14 %
Vitamin K	8 %	Magnesium	9 %
Vitamin B1	9 %	Zinc	9 %
Vitamin B2	10 %	Selenium	8 %
Niacin	3 %	Copper	11 %

OTHER BENEFICIAL NUTRIENTS (PER SERVING)

Choline	12 mg
Phytosterols	650 mg
ALA	100 mg

Nutrition Information

Serving Size **½ Pear** Servings **4**

Calories	**183**	Potassium	**217 mg**
Calories from fat	**81**	Total Carbohydrates	**25 g**
Total Fat	**9 g**	Dietary Fiber	**7 g**
Cholesterol	**0 mg**	Sugars	**15 g**
Sodium	**16 mg**	Protein	**3 g**
Vitamin C	**10 %**	Vitamin B6	**4 %**
Calcium	**5 %**	Folic Acid	**4 %**
Iron	**4 %**	Phosphorus	**10 %**
Vitamin E	**22 %**	Magnesium	**15 %**
Vitamin K	**5 %**	Zinc	**7 %**
Vitamin B1	**4 %**	Selenium	**1 %**
Vitamin B2	**15 %**	Copper	**27 %**
Niacin	**5 %**		

OTHER BENEFICIAL NUTRIENTS (PER SERVING)

Choline	**13 mg**
Phytosterols	**975 mg**

GREEN TEA POACHED PEARS

4 Pieces • Prep Time: 30 minutes • Poaching Time: 20 minutes • Medium

The French usually poach the pears in vanilla sugar syrup, but instead I poach the pear Andrew's healthy and zero-calorie Jasmine-Infused Green Tea. Any pears will work as long they are almost ripe, but still firm. In France, this is served with whipped cream. Feel free to our Coconut Cream [page 43].

---

1 vanilla bean, split in half
6 cups water
3 sachets of Andrew's Own Jasmine Green Tea
1 tbsp. of honey
1 tbsp. sliced ginger
2 firm, ripe pears with stem
½ cup sliced almonds
12 raspberries
6 pieces ChocoNuvo

---

1. Split the vanilla bean pod and scrape out the seeds so they can easily be distributed.
2. Bring the water to a boil in a saucepan and lower the heat. Add the vanilla bea tea bags, honey and sliced ginger, and let steep for 10 minutes.
3. Peel the pears. Remove the bottom with a small melon scoop. Carefully cut t pears in half, keeping the stem intact.
4. Poach the pears in the steeping water over low heat for 20 minutes. Place a rou piece of parchment paper on top of the pan to keep the pears from floating the surface.
5. Melt the ChocoNuvo for 1 minute in the microwave. Mix with a spatula. Place h a pear on each serving plate and garnish with raspberries. Drizzle the melt ChocoNuvo on top and decorate with sliced almonds. Serve immediately.

ROSES DES SABLES ("SAND ROSES")

About 14 Pieces • Prep Time: 10 minutes • Cooling Time: 1 Hour • Easy

This is a delicious treat that is quick and easy to make. You can add any nuts you like, as long as you crush them. If this recipe is too large, feel free to cut it in half. You can also sprinkle some healthy Matcha green tea powder, or a pinch of turmeric for another healthy addition!

---

8 pieces ChocoNuvo

1 cup mixed assorted dried fruits, nuts or seeds (such as pumpkin seeds, pine nuts, raisins, dried cherries, sliced almonds, goji berries, etc.)

14 mini muffin liners

---

1 In a skillet, on medium to high heat, roast nuts and seeds for 5 minutes. Make sure you watch them closely so they don't burn. Remove from the heat and mix them in a bowl with the dried fruits.

2 Melt the ChocoNuvo for 1 minute in the microwave, and mix well with the dried fruits and nuts. Reserve a few sliced almonds and goji berries to decorate on top, if you wish.

3 Place 1 tsp. (or a little more) of the mixture in each muffin liner. They should not be too perfect so they truly look like sand roses! Makes 14 pieces, but may vary.

4 Refrigerate for a minimum of 1 hour. You can freeze them too. Decorate with a sliced almond and a dried Goji berry on top.

Nutrition Information

Serving Size **1 Piece** Servings **14**

Calories	**56**	Potassium	**70 mg**
Calories from fat	**36**	Total Carbohydrates	**6 g**
Total Fat	**4 g**	Dietary Fiber	**1 g**
Cholesterol	**0 mg**	Sugars	**3 g**
Sodium	**18 mg**	Protein	**1 g**
Calcium	**1 %**	Vitamin B6	**2 %**
Iron	**1 %**	Folic Acid	**1 %**
Vitamin E	**4 %**	Phosphorus	**3 %**
Vitamin K	**3 %**	Magnesium	**4 %**
Vitamin B1	**1 %**	Zinc	**3 %**
Vitamin B2	**2 %**	Selenium	**1 %**
Niacin	**2 %**	Copper	**9 %**

OTHER BENEFICIAL NUTRIENTS (PER SERVING)

Choline	**2 mg**
Phytosterols	**371 mg**

CAULIFLOWER AND SHISHITO PEPPER

6 Side Dishes • Prep Time: 25 minutes • Cooking Time: 20 minutes • Easy

This is a wonderful way to combine ChocoNuvo with vegetables! My girlfrier April, inspired this creation, since she loves to make savory and chocolatey dish for her sons, Maverick and Lord. In Spain, they also mix Ancho chiles and differe warm spices and peppers with chocolate. I use red hot chili flakes because th are easier. This dish is also inspired by the cuisine I grew up eating when my fam visited Northern Spain each summer.

---

1 head cauliflower, cut into small florets

3 to 4 tbsp. olive oil

kosher salt & pepper

1 tsp. red hot chili flakes

15 shishito peppers

1 shallot, minced

2 cloves garlic, crushed

2 tbsp. sherry

4 pieces ChocoNuvo plus 1 piece shaved

⅓ cup toasted, sliced almonds

½ cup queso fresco (crumbled)

3 sprigs oregano

(Continued next pag

Nutrition Information

Serving Size **1 Dish** Servings **6**

Calories	**212**	Potassium	**660 mg**
Calories from fat	**126**	Total Carbohydrates	**17 g**
Total Fat	**14 g**	Dietary Fiber	**7 g**
Cholesterol	**8 mg**	Sugars	**7 g**
Sodium	**146 mg**	Protein	**7 g**
Vitamin A	**9 %**	Niacin	**11 %**
Vitamin C	**236 %**	Vitamin B6	**46 %**
Calcium	**13 %**	Folic Acid	**19 %**
Iron	**8 %**	Vitamin B12	**8 %**
Vitamin D	**2 %**	Phosphorus	**22 %**
Vitamin E	**22 %**	Magnesium	**17 %**
Vitamin K	**38 %**	Zinc	**12 %**
Vitamin B1	**15 %**	Selenium	**6 %**
Vitamin B2	**18 %**	Copper	**24 %**

OTHER BENEFICIAL NUTRIENTS (PER SERVING)

Choline	**58 mg**
Phytosterols	**542 mg**

CAULIFLOWER AND SHISHITO PEPPERS

(Continued from previous page.)

1 Preheat the oven to 400°. Coat the cauliflower florets with 2 tbsp. olive oil and season with salt, pepper and red hot chili flakes. Bake for 15 minutes on a baking sheet lined with foil.

2 In a large skillet over high heat, add the remaining olive oil and sauté the shishito peppers for 5 minutes, until their skin starts bursting. Remove them from the heat and place on a paper towel.

3 Sauté the minced shallots with the crushed garlic for 2 to 3 minutes, until translucent. Add the sherry and the 4 pieces of ChocoNuvo. Make sure everything melts nicely together and add a little red hot chili flakes, if you wish.

4 Place the grilled cauliflower and shishito peppers on your serving platter. Sprinkle the queso fresco on top and drizzle the ChocoNuvo/sherry sauce. Top with almonds and fresh oregano. Shave the remaining ChocoNuvo with a vegetable peeler and place the shavings on top.

Chicken MoleNuvo

4 Servings • Prep Time: 20 minutes • Cooking Time: 25 minutes • Medium to Difficu

I always thought that classic chicken mole would be very time consuming, but that is not the ca at all. This recipe is quick, efficient and absolutely delicious! I use peanut butter, but you can u any nut butter you choose. Andrew loves pecan butter. I chose dried apricots, but raisins a work very well. I used clementines here because I did not have oranges or orange juice an always enjoy working with clementines when they are available and in season. Most chicken m has a very smooth sauce, but that is an option as an extra step if you choose. See what you pref

---

4 small chicken breasts
½ tsp. salt
½ tsp. pepper
½ sprig coriander
½ tsp. cumin
1 tsp. ancho chile powder
6-7 clementines
1 tbsp. peanut oil (or olive oil works well)
clementine or orange zest

1 shallot
2 cloves garlic
⅓ cup dried apricots or raisins
1 cup low sodium chicken broth
2 tbsp. peanut butter
5 pieces ChocoNuvo
¼ cup sliced, roasted almonds
A few sprigs fresh cilantro

(Continued next pag

CHICKEN MOLENUVO

(Continued from previous page.)

1 Season the chicken: rub the coriander, cumin and ½ tsp. of the ancho chile onto the chicken. Sprinkle with the salt and pepper.

2 Juice enough clementines to make ¾ cup of juice. Reserve.

3 In a large skillet or medium braiser (similar to a Dutch oven) over medium/high heat, add the peanut oil and sauté the chicken for 4 minutes on each side until crispy and golden. Transfer the chicken to a plate and let it rest.

4 Chop the shallots and garlic, and sauté in the skillet or braiser over medium heat for 3 minutes, until translucent. Add the chopped, dried apricots and the peanut butter, and mix well with a spatula. Add the rest of the ancho chile and the ChocoNuvo and mix well. Add the chicken broth and clementine juice. Reduce the heat to simmer for 5 minutes. Add the chicken back to the sauce and cook all together for 10 more minutes to get the delicious flavor.

5 This sauce can be placed in the blender for 1 minute to make it smooth, as an option.

6 Place the chicken on a plate, top with the sauce and sprinkle with roasted almonds, a few slices of clementines and fresh cilantro. You can serve it with a side of beans and rice and some shaved ChocoNuvo on top!

Nutrition Information

Serving Size **1 Chicken Breast** Servings **4**

Nutrient	Amount	Nutrient	Amount
Calories	**441**	Potassium	**824 mg**
Calories from fat	**171**	Total Carbohydrates	**32 g**
Total Fat	**19 g**	Dietary Fiber	**7 g**
Cholesterol	**84 mg**	Sugars	**22 g**
Sodium	**444 mg**	Protein	**38 g**

Nutrient	Amount	Nutrient	Amount
Vitamin A	**12 %**	Niacin	**119 %**
Vitamin C	**47 %**	Vitamin B6	**62 %**
Calcium	**11 %**	Folic Acid	**10 %**
Iron	**14 %**	Vitamin B12	**16 %**
Vitamin D	**1 %**	Phosphorus	**52 %**
Vitamin E	**32 %**	Magnesium	**30 %**
Vitamin K	**6 %**	Zinc	**23 %**
Vitamin B1	**15 %**	Selenium	**52 %**
Vitamin B2	**28 %**	Copper	**37 %**

OTHER BENEFICIAL NUTRIENTS (PER SERVING)

Choline	**115 mg**
Phytosterols	**813 mg**

Triple ChocoNuvo Turkey Chil

About 14 Cups • Prep Time: 20 minutes • Cooking Time: about 1 Hour • Medium

Definitely not your average chili, as the ChocoNuvo and chocolate beer bring unexpec richness to this exceptional chili. One of the favorite recipes in my first cookbook cover Andrew's Favorite Soups was our Turkey Chili. This recipe adds some serious depth, darkn and flavor to Andrew's Favorite Chili. I used all three chocolate intensities. The meat can replaced with ground beef, chicken or veal, but turkey is Andrew's favorite, so I thought it perfect here. I also found this chocolate stout beer, but you can use any beer you like (or non all – replace with more stock instead). If you do not like it spicy, you can replace the ancho c or chili powder with paprika, it will be less tasty though. If it's too thick, you might want to a extra chicken or turkey broth. Queso fresco is a great alternative to the sharp cheddar chee For extra flavor, you may add 4 pieces of turkey bacon cut in small pieces (in step 1).

---

2 tbsp. olive oil

1 red onion, finely chopped

1 yellow pepper (1 cup chopped)

1 orange pepper (1 cup chopped)

4 cloves garlic, crushed

1 tbsp. cumin

1 tsp. cinnamon

1 tbsp. ancho chile or chili powder + 1 tsp red hot chili flakes

4 cups cooked, ground turkey meat (1½ lbs)

3 cans beans: black beans, pinto beans and red beans, rinsed

1 can diced tomatoes (15 oz.)

1 cup cherry tomatoes, halves

2 tbsp. tomato paste

1 cup chocolate stout beer

1½ cups chicken or turkey stock

Salt and pepper, to taste

8 pieces ChocoNuvo (a mix of the 91%, 74% and 66%)

1 oz. fresh scallions

Serve with:

⅔ cup extra sharp white cheddar or Queso fresco (optional)

½ cup fat free sour cream (optional)

1 lime, cut in wedges

(Continued next pag

TRIPLE CHOCONUVO TURKEY CHILI

(Continued from previous page.)

1 In a quart soup pot, over medium heat, warm the olive oil then add the onion and the chopped peppers, stirring until golden, about 5 minutes.

2 Add the crushed garlic, cumin, cinnamon, ancho chile or chili powder and red hot chili flakes and stir for an additional 2 minutes.

3 Add the turkey, rinsed beans, tomatoes (fresh and canned), tomato paste, the chocolate stout beer, broth, salt and pepper and bring to a boil. Reduce the heat and let it simmer for 50 minutes.

4 Add the ChocoNuvo and the chopped scallions, reserving some for garnish, and stir well for 3 minutes.

5 Ladle into individual bowls, garnish and serve with the shredded sharp cheddar (or Queso fresco) and sour cream, if you wish. Place a lime wedge on the side of the bowl. I sometimes decorate with sliced avocado.

Nutrition Information

Serving Size **1 Cup** Servings **14**

Calories	**221**	Potassium	**573 mg**
Calories from fat	**72**	Total Carbohydrates	**22 g**
Total Fat	**8 g**	Dietary Fiber	**8 g**
Cholesterol	**38 mg**	Sugars	**4 g**
Sodium	**238 mg**	Protein	**16 g**
Vitamin A	**8 %**	Vitamin B6	**31 %**
Vitamin C	**55 %**	Folic Acid	**13 %**
Calcium	**8 %**	Vitamin B12	**28 %**
Iron	**17 %**	Phosphorus	**29 %**
Vitamin E	**10 %**	Magnesium	**17 %**
Vitamin K	**9 %**	Zinc	**26 %**
Vitamin B1	**29 %**	Selenium	**23 %**
Vitamin B2	**19 %**	Copper	**32 %**
Niacin	**28 %**		

OTHER BENEFICIAL NUTRIENTS (PER SERVING)

Choline	**59 mg**
Phytosterols	**371 mg**

SWEET POTATO CHIPS

25 Pieces • Prep Time: 10 minutes • Cooking Time: 15 minutes • Medium

I have always enjoyed chocolate with spices and chili, so I thought it would be great to include simple recipe of healthy sweet potato chips with ChocoNuvo and healthy spices. Andrew a love extra virgin olive oil and we do not hesitate to use it abundantly in our kitchen. Depend if you like your chips crispier, bake them for another 5 minutes if you wish.

- 1 sweet potato
- ½ tbsp. extra virgin olive oil
- ½ tbsp. chili oil
- A pinch of sea salt & pepper
- 1 tsp. red hot chili flakes or cayenne pepper
- 1 tsp. turmeric
- 4 pieces ChocoNuvo

---

1. Preheat the oven to 400°. Line a baking sheet with parchment paper or foil.
2. Slice the sweet potato very thin using a mandolin or, if you use a knife, make about ⅛ inch thick.
3. In a medium bowl, add the olive oil and chili oil to the sweet potato slices. To until the potato slices are coated. Add the sea salt, pepper, turmeric and red h chili flakes or cayenne.
4. Place on a single layer on the baking sheet. Bake until browned and crispy, abo 15 minutes. I rotate the baking sheet halfway through, for even baking.
5. Melt the ChocoNuvo for 1 minute in the microwave and dip the tip of the chip it. Place on a piece of parchment paper. You may sprinkle some extra sea salt top! Enjoy immediately!

Nutrition Information

Serving Size **5 Pieces** Servings **5**

Calories	73	Potassium	156 mg
Calories from fat	36	Total Carbohydrates	8 g
Total Fat	4 g	Dietary Fiber	2 g
Cholesterol	0 mg	Sugars	3 g
Sodium	136 mg	Protein	1 g
Vitamin A	41 %	Niacin	3 %
Vitamin C	8 %	Vitamin B6	8 %
Calcium	1 %	Folic Acid	1 %
Iron	2 %	Phosphorus	3 %
Vitamin E	5 %	Magnesium	3 %
Vitamin K	3 %	Zinc	2 %
Vitamin B1	3 %	Copper	6 %
Vitamin B2	3 %		

OTHER BENEFICIAL NUTRIENTS (PER SERVING)

Choline	4 mg
Phytosterols	520 mg

Nutrition Information

Serving Size **1 Piece** Servings **15**

Calories	**108**	Potassium	**76 mg**
Calories from fat	**81**	Total Carbohydrates	**7 g**
Total Fat	**9 g**	Dietary Fiber	**2 g**
Cholesterol	**0 mg**	Sugars	**3 g**
Sodium	**30 mg**	Protein	**2 g**
Calcium	**3 %**	Folic Acid	**3 %**
Iron	**2 %**	Phosphorus	**7 %**
Vitamin E	**16 %**	Magnesium	**9 %**
Vitamin B1	**2 %**	Zinc	**4 %**
Vitamin B2	**10 %**	Selenium	**1 %**
Niacin	**3 %**	Copper	**11 %**
Vitamin B6	**1 %**		

OTHER BENEFICIAL NUTRIENTS (PER SERVING)

Choline	**6 mg**
Phytosterols	**867 mg**

ALMOND BUTTER CUPS WITH SEA SALT

About 15 Pieces • Prep Time: 20 minutes • Cooling Time: 40 minutes • Medium

This is my version of "Peanut Butter Cups," but Andrew insists that almond butter is a much healthier version. Any nut butter would work, and you can then top with matching nuts (or any nuts). If you find this recipe too large and perhaps too expensive, please reduce it in half. These can be kept frozen up to a month.

Coconut oil spray
20 pieces ChocoNuvo
1 tsp. coconut oil (or ghee)
½ cup almond butter
1 tbsp. agave or honey
3 tbsp. almond or quinoa flour (use any flour you like)
15 raw almonds to decorate
A pinch of sea salt
About 15 mini muffin liners

---

1 Place paper liners in a muffin tin and lightly spray with oil. You can use a silicon mold, if you wish.

2 Melt the ChocoNuvo in the microwave with the coconut oil for 1 minute and mix with a spatula. Place 1 tsp. of the melted ChocoNuvo mixture in each muffin liner. Freeze for 10 minutes.

3 In a medium bowl, mix the nut butter, agave and flour with a fork or your hands (I wear gloves, it gets messy), until it forms a hard paste. If the almond butter is particularly thick, you can add a tsp. of coconut oil.

4 Take approximately 1 tsp. of paste and use your hand to make a firm ball, flattening it a little before placing it on the top of the frozen chocolate in the muffin liner. Repeat until all the paste is gone.

5 Pour approximately 1 tsp. of melted ChocoNuvo on top of the contents of each muffin liner to make your small Almond Butter Cup. Decorate with 1 almond and a few grains of sea salt. Place in the freezer for 30 minutes minimum.

GAIL'S MINI CHEESECAKE WITH COOKIE CRUST

24 Mini Cheesecakes • Prep Time: 30 minutes • Baking Time: 25 minutes • Mediur

Andrew's sister, Gail, gave me this simple, yet delicious cheesecake recipe. But since ev the healthiest of cheesecakes can be calorically rich and thus, must be treated with respec chose to make this as a portion-controlled, mini-cheesecake. I use the 1/3-fat cream cheese a although the recipe can also work with fat free cream cheese, it just isn't as smooth. I mixed l of the cream cheese with melted ChocoNuvo for a marbled look! I added a little raspberry top of each little cheesecake, but you could also add your favorite fruit or melt some ChocoNu and drizzle it with a spoon for a "zebra" effect. Delicious!

Crust:

Coconut oil spray

6 Chouette Oatmeal Cookies *(page 25)*

1 tbsp. agave

2 dates

1 tsp. cinnamon

1 tbsp. coconut oil

Filling:

8 oz. ⅓ fat cream cheese

2 tbsp. fat free sour cream

2 tbsp. corn starch

1 tsp. vanilla extract

2 tbsp. sugar

2 eggs (or 4 egg whites)

6 pieces ChocoNuvo

(Continued next pag

GAIL'S MINI CHEESECAKE WITH COOKIE CRUST

Nutrition Information

Serving Size **1 Mini Cheesecake** Servings **24**

Calories	**75**	Potassium	**43 mg**
Calories from fat	**36**	Total Carbohydrates	**8 g**
Total Fat	**4 g**	Dietary Fiber	**1 g**
Cholesterol	**19 mg**	Sugars	**4 g**
Sodium	**73 mg**	Protein	**2 g**

Vitamin A	**3 %**	Vitamin B6	**1 %**
Calcium	**3 %**	Folic Acid	**3 %**
Iron	**1 %**	Vitamin B12	**6 %**
Vitamin D	**1 %**	Phosphorus	**4 %**
Vitamin E	**1 %**	Magnesium	**1 %**
Vitamin K	**1 %**	Zinc	**2 %**
Vitamin B1	**2 %**	Selenium	**4 %**
Vitamin B2	**5 %**	Copper	**2 %**
Niacin	**1 %**		

OTHER BENEFICIAL NUTRIENTS (PER SERVING)

Choline	**13 mg**
Phytosterols	**230 mg**

(Continued from previous page.)

1. Preheat the oven to 350°. Place paper liners in a mini-muffin tin and very lightly spray with oil.

2. Combine the cookies, agave, dates, cinnamon and coconut oil in a food processor, mixing well until it forms a dough.

3. Press 1 tbsp. of dough into each paper liner.

4. In a medium bowl, mix the cream cheese, sour cream, corn starch, vanilla extract and sugar. Once the mixture is nice and smooth, add one egg at a time.

5. Melt the 6 pieces of ChocoNuvo in the microwave for 1 minute. Divide the cream cheese mixture into 2 bowls, mixing the melted ChocoNuvo in one of the bowls of cream cheese mixture. Combine each half of the cream cheese mixture (the regular and the "chocolatey" one) so you get a lovely "Black & White" effect!

6. Divide the marbled mixture evenly between the muffin liners (about ½ tbsp. in each) and bake for 25 minutes maximum. Serve with a raspberry on top.

Chloe's Granola Parfait

4 Parfaits • Prep Time: 6 minutes • Easy

Andrew's adorable niece, Chloe, loves her Granola Parfait for breakfast, so I just had to mak a version with ChocoNuvo. I sometimes use dried fruits, and it is delicious with a lovely fru compote. You can also add a little shredded coconut on top, drizzle maple syrup or some melte ChocoNuvo. Our granola recipe is in our **"Oat"standing Recipes** *booklet.*

- 1 cup + ⅓ cup granola
- 4 + 2 pieces ChocoNuvo
- ½ tbsp. flaxseeds
- ½ tbsp. chia seeds
- 1 cup fresh strawberries
- 1 dragon fruit
- 1 cup plain, nonfat yogurt

---

1. Mix the granola with 4 pieces of crushed ChocoNuvo, the flaxseeds and chia seec If you have more time, you can toast the granola for 3 to 5 minutes in the oven 375°, then add the crushed ChocoNuvo and let it melt within the granola. YUM!

2. Cut the strawberries and the dragon fruit into small pieces. I use cookie cutte for the dragon fruit, to make it prettier.

3. In a mason jar or small bowl, place alternating layers of ⅓ cup of granola, ⅓ cup yogurt and ⅔ cup of fruit. Shave the extra ChocoNuvo with a vegetable peeler the top of the parfait. If you wish, add a tsp. of Coconut Cream *(page 43)* to decora

Nutrition Information

Serving Size **1 Parfait** Servings **4**

Calories	**315**	Potassium	**452 mg**
Calories from fat	**126**	Total Carbohydrates	**36 g**
Total Fat	**14 g**	Dietary Fiber	**8 g**
Cholesterol	**1 mg**	Sugars	**19 g**
Sodium	**58 mg**	Protein	**11 g**
Vitamin C	**38 %**	Vitamin B6	**14 %**
Calcium	**18 %**	Folic Acid	**13 %**
Iron	**12 %**	Vitamin B12	**16 %**
Vitamin E	**31 %**	Phosphorus	**45 %**
Vitamin K	**5 %**	Magnesium	**32 %**
Vitamin B1	**34 %**	Zinc	**30 %**
Vitamin B2	**25 %**	Selenium	**27 %**
Niacin	**9 %**	Copper	**35 %**

Other Beneficial Nutrients (per serving)

Choline	**32 mg**
Phytosterols	**975 mg**
ALA	**900 mg**

DIPPED FROZEN BANANAS WITH GOJI BERRIES

4 Mini Treats • Prep Time: 5 minutes • Cooling Time: Overnight • Very Easy

Bananas are among the most popular fruits on Earth and this is a fun, super-simple recipe for them. In fact it is so simple, I almost overlooked it, but I like it so much I had to include it. On their own, bananas are a healthy snack and once you freeze them overnight, all you do is dip them in ChocoNuvo and decorate.

---

1 banana, sliced

4 pieces ChocoNuvo

¼ cup goji berries, crushed nuts or sprinkles

4 or 5 toothpicks

---

1. Cut banana into 4 or 5 pieces and freeze overnight in a sealed bag.

2. Melt the ChocoNuvo for 1 minute in a small bowl or cup. Place your toothpick on the end of each banana piece. Dip in the ChocoNuvo.

3. Place the goji berries, ice cream sprinkles, shaved ChocoNuvo or crushed nuts on freshly dipped banana. Voila! Keep in the freezer!!!

Nutrition Information

Serving Size **¼ Banana** — Servings **4**

Calories	**74**	Potassium	**109 mg**
Calories from fat	**18**	Total Carbohydrates	**13 g**
Total Fat	**2 g**	Dietary Fiber	**2 g**
Cholesterol	**0 mg**	Sugars	**8 g**
Sodium	**14 mg**	Protein	**1 g**
Vitamin C	**3 %**	Folic Acid	**1 %**
Iron	**1 %**	Phosphorus	**1 %**
Vitamin B1	**1 %**	Magnesium	**3 %**
Vitamin B2	**2 %**	Zinc	**1 %**
Niacin	**1 %**	Selenium	**1 %**
Vitamin B6	**8 %**	Copper	**3 %**

OTHER BENEFICIAL NUTRIENTS (PER SERVING)

Choline	**3 mg**
Phytosterols	**650 mg**

SWEET CASHEW PASTE / "MYLK"

2 ½ Cups • Prep Time: 5 minutes • Soaking Time: Overnight • Easy

We make this Sweet Cashew Paste to create delicious, rich fruit bowls and smoothies, or to m our own "Mylk". The Mylk is lovely to use with our Ultimate Oatmeal and Ultimate Oat Bran sometimes you just need a spoon to enjoy it!

Sweet Cashew Paste:

2 cups raw cashews, soaked overnight or a minimum of 3 hours

1 tbsp. agave or honey

2 dates (pitted)

1 scoop Ultimate PC + Phosphatidyl Choline Liver & Brain Granules

4 capsules Ultimate Friendly Flora

1 tsp. cinnamon

1 tbsp. vanilla extract

1 cup water or coconut water (you will need more for the Mylk)

---

1. Place the cups of cashews in a bowl and cover with water. Place a plastic wrap ov it and refrigerate overnight.
2. Make the paste: Mix everything for the recipe in the blender until smooth. Add little water if needed and always refrigerate. It can also be frozen up to a mon

MYLK

1. Add 4 cups of water to the paste and blend until EXTREMELY smooth. You c pass the Mylk through a milk bag to make it smoother, but I never do.

Nutrition Information

Serving Size **¼ Cup** Servings **10**

Calories	178	Potassium	167 mg
Calories from fat	117	Total Carbohydrates	12 g
Total Fat	13 g	Dietary Fiber	1 g
Cholesterol	0 mg	Sugars	4 g
Sodium	6 mg	Protein	4 g
Calcium	2 %	Vitamin B6	6 %
Iron	9 %	Folic Acid	5 %
Vitamin E	2 %	Phosphorus	19 %
Vitamin K	11 %	Magnesium	23 %
Vitamin B1	5 %	Zinc	19 %
Vitamin B2	6 %	Selenium	6 %
Niacin	3 %	Copper	68 %

OTHER BENEFICIAL NUTRIENTS (PER SERVING)

Choline .... 58 mg

COCONUT CREAM

About 2 Cups • Prep Time: 5 minutes • Cooling Time: Overnight • Very Easy

This is the wonderful topping for our Frozen Hot Cocoa (page 12) and can also be used as a topping for any of our other mini desserts. 1 tsp. per serving is all you need.

---

1 can coconut milk (Turned upside down in the fridge overnight)

1 tbsp. agave nectar

1 tsp. vanilla extract

---

1 Turn the can upside down in the fridge overnight. Once the can is cold, scoop out the thick coconut part and use the left-over coconut water for smoothie.

2 In a cold bowl, mix with an electric mixer: the creamy thick coconut milk, (not the watery milk), with the agave and the vanilla extract, until it forms a whipped cream. Refrigerate until you are ready to use.

Nutrition Information

Serving Size **1 tsp.**		Servings **42**	
Calories	**15**	Potassium	**15 mg**
Calories from fat	**9**	Total Carbohydrates	**1 g**
Total Fat	**1 g**	Dietary Fiber	**0 g**
Cholesterol	**0 mg**	Sugars	**1 g**
Sodium	**1 mg**	Protein	**0 g**
Iron	**1 %**	Selenium	**1 %**
Phosphorus	**1 %**	Copper	**2 %**
Magnesium	**1 %**		

OTHER BENEFICIAL NUTRIENTS (PER SERVING)

Choline .... **1 mg**

Lincoln's Corner